Employed

Also by James Bertolino:

NORTHWEST POETS Anthology, Editor
1968 Quixote Press

DAY OF CHANGE, 1968 Gunrunner Press

DROOL, 1968 Quixote Press

MR. NOBODY, 1969 Ox Head Press

CEREMONY, 1969 Morgan Press

STONE-MARROW, 1969 Anachoreta Press
(trade edition: Abraxas Press)

BECOMING HUMAN, 1970 Road Runner Press

EDGING THROUGH, 1972 Lillabulero Press

(in manuscript)

MAKING SPACE FOR OUR LIVING

THE LIBERATION CLINIC

EMPLOYED / poems

James Bertolino

an ithaca house book  Ithaca

Many of these poems have appeared previously in Abraxas, Ark River Review, Cafe Solo, Cold Duck, Concerning Poetry, Cottonwood Review, Crazy Horse, Doones, The Dragonfly, Driftwood, Foxfire, Galley Sail Review, The Goodly Co., Hey Lady, Human Voice, The Intro/5 Anthology, Mandala, Mojo Navigator(e), Northwest Review, The Oregonian, Ox Head 8, The Poetry Bag, Quartet, Quixote, Red Cedar Review, Road Apple Review, Sage, Stinktree, Suction, Trace, and Wisconsin Review.

The poems "Under Mayan Sun," "Notes For An Elegy," and "Snow Angel" (under the title "A Seasonal Poem") first appeared in Poetry.

A number of these poems (often earlier versions) were included in limited-edition pamphlets by Quixote Press, Abraxas Press and Road Runner Press.

ISBN 0-87886-016-9

ITHACA HOUSE
314 FOREST HOME DRIVE
ITHACA, NEW YORK 14850

CONTENTS

CONTENTS

two/THE EXECUTRIX OF WEIRDS

three/THE EMPTY BREAD-BOX HAS A RED EDGE

TAKE THESE SYLLABLES

Sting
into
this poem.
Take these syllables
where they hang
like fruit
& twist them, pull towards you till
something, a shape
comes

        a sun-bright tomato red
        & yellow on the inside juice
        runs down the forearm

sour   then
sweet
as the rejoicing tissues spill
furrows
          through the tongue

& the thought of it
tickles

& stings

one/EMPLOYED

for Lois

THE RED DRESS

The whirr
of the sewing machine

her back
        bent
beautiful in the tension
of her toil

the purr
of my thread
              between
her fingers

brings her to me,
brings us,
weaves me in the house
of her

& nowhere
is there stronger
more soft
          fabric
than this

THE NIGHT WAS SMOOTH

Sure the night was smooth
as milkweed silk
against the fingers,
& the wet rags just washed
were warm;
even the doctor's rough farm hands
had knowing, were good.
There was a confidence.

But the baby wasn't right.

ELEGY

1.

Old Growley died this year.
They pushed his
rotten wood trailer
over the rim of the dump
where he presided
as long as I can remember.
The men took Squeaks,
his grim little dog,
away too.

2.

A bent woman
who itched her chin
on her knee
as she walked, & slept
on the cold Courthouse steps
(except in winter...I don't know where
she slept then),
doesn't feed the pigeons
anymore &
they've flown to the park
where musty old men
attempt to fool them
with cigar-butts.

3.

A green Mack truck
(with no trailer)
bore down upon a preoccupied
wren,
& before the feathers
had settled,
three sparrows &
the rest
of the wrens
were singing again.

LOOSE THE REINS

Whisper to the ear
of the broken blue horse
...dance...dance
let cracked hooves shudder
over the cruel grass
of years

Wince
to notes
of an off-key calliope,
let memory come
in fool-
fits
& starts

It's bad limbs
& sweat,
it's pains in the chest
bring the sawdust secret
you quietly held
but could never admit:

The calliope wheezed
& the horses
were old.

EVE OF JULY FOURTH

A hound twitches
with the sound
of vomit
as a party breaks up

Two people make it
without love
on dry, desperate ground

Alone
a child weeps
as bats whisper past
her damp pillow

In the red buzz
of an emergency flare
an old man punishes
furiously
a mosquito
                his sun-tanned

grandson
hunts nightcrawlers
on his knees
in the dark
                eyes aglint

with silver-
speckled fish

& fireworks

SUNDAY MORNING

A squirrel's
entrails
adorn
my black-top drive

old crimes
brought to light

They steam
& are fanned
by a halo of drowned nightcrawlers

kept juicy
in the sun
by pools of rain

MEMORIAL PARK AT SUNRISE

On the damp grass
a sandwich
in a greasy brown bag

salami on dry rye
tired frills of lettuce
along its edge

creating a gentle resonance

with the snuffling
of the wino
on the bench

adrift in a dream of wheatfields
& sunlight

under a shifting paper canopy

of yesterday's
crime.

BEWARE

the poetry of
                    pinking
shears
sharecroppers
                    potsherds
honey-slaked
                    peers
skates
air
golden-spoked prayer
books
& Koala bears
that rub their noses
in the spice of
                        Spring

LONG HAIR MUSIC

My hair is so long
& shaggy
the little soft-legged
creatures
are raising their
scaly skirts
& giving birth
to shelled young hellions
that sneak around
the brown trees
& create
grave disturbances
with my dandruff.

ELEPHANT TREE

Bulky.
Thick grey bark.
Wrinkles circle the limbs.
The girth, the belly-trunk
breathes. It grows
ponderously.
Heavy veins run the length
to dark leaves.
When I go
it sulks.

TEACHING THE SUN

for Reneé

Outside the March wind
means business.
From a winter sky
grown old & grey
the snowflakes, white stragglers
work into dark crevices
& caves
of wet bark.
        The trees, trembling
shake black fists
            remembering with rage
their kidnapped leaves.

But wait.
A swirl
    a dance of red
setting fire to the lilac bushes
near the field, it's

a girl! lovely
    a whirl of laughter
teasing the sun
from its mask
of dull clouds

teaching the sun
to sing!

EMPLOYED

I quit my job this morning.

They couldn't understand
ducks
rippling across my mind
from shore to weeds & back
or down for grub.

What's more I didn't care
for their caring to keep me
behind a counter. Blue

moving into green on the hills
& the black snake
with red stripes the length of its body

stretch my eyes
beyond books

tell me I'm right,
I'm right.

A COOL DRINK

New buds brush
the window
minutes bend
around the scent
of hay: fluidly
the kittens, clover &
birds of the morning
become evening: blue water
through transparent
pipe

        the hours without war
thrill
the throat

THE CHORD

Morning dust &
my yawp
wearing to its thinnest
timbre   strokes
even now
the timorous motes
to spin   to color
to something brighter

to chord

Thus my fingers
stoke responses
in the morning air

Thus I pair my breath
with sun   fish   stream

POISON OAK POEMS

Monoliths

Six houses shimmering
white against
blue foothills
across the valley

exaggerate
the importance
of man.

Of Permanence

Fourteen goats
& a kid
make clear impressions
in slick
brown mud

telling more
to posterity than

three lambs
soft
in a field crazy
with flowers

Design

Worms hole
flower petals
with composition

the sun
free
below.

Flight Pattern

The ridiculous clatter
of three fat geese
sweating
to get into the air

makes me wonder
if only man
was meant to fly.

OREGON SUMMER

Cold mornings stalk
sun

sun beats stalks
to green

greens
bloom

The precarious color
of bamboo
shoots skyward

a yellow-green rocket
trails leaves

A blue-jay's skree
slides under the brush
like a meteor

&
rain

ROOM

The bowl-shaped
wicker chair
                    the fine

contour
of narrow-necked vase

the smoldering edges
of red
   red dahlias

                         pucker

the air

& you

blue veins (your
delicate
                  charge
your nipples

your thoughts reach
hold
like a bowl

                         my space

MOSCOW SONG

The scarab beetle
its glow
in paint on the stone
charges
the room

makes passionate words with
the purple &
red-striped tunic, the polka-dot panties
flung wild
to the floor

Outside the window
Jennifer picks wonder-seeds
from the gutter

while Spru, his thigh
brushing lightly
her curved back

strums
a mountain dulcimer

with splayed fingers
touches
the wind

I TAKE THEE

I take thee
woman
where ruby-eyed fish
fire
the waters of night

Where delicate indigo birds
roost
till dawn

then trellis
the amber flesh of morning

over yearlings
brash
for cool mountain air

& the wordless heights
of blood

AS IF BOUND

In a field
the summer grass thick
& short
slope stubbled grey
with boulders
some larger than
the roofs of old cars

you notice
the birds
whether alone or in flocks
coming over
                    dip
with the hill

your own eyesight seems
to bow towards
those boulders
when you would look beyond
to the fine oaks
near the creek

& is it perhaps
that they alone have gone
the distance you
are the first mile of

that they in their cool shapes
hold everything's
right name?

ONTO THE SAME ROCK

There is a lull
in the crickets

A ruffled thrush
in the crotch
of an elm

notices the calm
covering its beak
with trembling wing   Now the weak-
est limb

shatters the air with
green

spills a cream-
colored egg
onto the same rock

split
by the yellow
flash the

lightning

THE RITUAL

Dawn heaves
a red lance
to cannibal desert.

From mud-plaster ruins
I whoop!
crazed shaman
hankering
to dance the ghost cactus.

My mad limbs
beat a dust drum,
surf of subsoil breakers
in a landlocked sea.

& as night shrieks,
cairn of black stones,
home to my lover

my dogfaced squaw
with her creel
of dried fish.

WHEN I HOLD

to your shoulders
with heavy fingers

& down an eyelash roll a tear
to break on your brow

it doesn't matter
that sorcerers dance on their drums
when you pass

& neighbors call you witch.

ELECTRIC BLOOD or
WELL-PRUNED SAGE SURROUNDS THE TIPI

Dining noisily
& with relish

he spoke to his family
the tribe
& to his wizened mongrel:

The kiss of the witch be on you!

Let the blood of stones
irrigate
the fatty tissue of your brains!

From that moment forth
he gave his life to the Poem.

Life is easy
he said,
simple as wind
through a small girl's fingers.

A kind of tingle when you think.

A familiar.

THE OLD CLEARING

With purpose
the sun silky
through gauze curtains
strings drawn   a gentle force
the morning draws me   here
place I've never   off dusty road
under carefully the
barbed-wire
miles from how I've walked here
my thoughts
a silk force

feet bare to grass / bare too the
Indian
is here now   not with me / with

trees   my place
at the far side the field
a gentle web this
old clearing
him   my place shimmering weeds
so warm
sun's kiss
soft net this old
Indian silk
embrace

UNDER MAYAN SUN

Yellow
crushed meat of
dried fruit
forms islands
in blood
            lady bugs
swim
on flat stone.

The ritual dances
have ceased.

   I cross
hand
over hand
my single nerve stretched taut
to where your
virgin gold
               breasts
heave no more.

Spring.

This rite of maize
your blood
will grow tall
                    & thoughtless
as blades.

My love
for you
was a fall of bones.

MAIZE

The cold humus,
the dark crystals mocking
twist
human breath
to mold.

Then seasons lull.
The dull genes,
our huddled trolls
grasp for light:
crystals crack,
the silt flows.

Now entering the stalks,
scraped to sap
by possibilities,

we feel yellow
greening, growing about
us, gloving
the knobbed

shaft, smothering
our only un-
pigmented roots

with color: answering
the last
question, forbidding us

to die.

BEYOND THE STORM

The storm has come again today,
it rages shrill pins.
I hear a pale child
moaning alone
by the bottom rocks of the field.
I feel the blowing wet
bruise her face.

Three days have been
since Marlys left
in her wool coat, winding
down the fright of the path, dark.
The branches are knives.
Out of lulling wind comes quacking,
a duck on the raft.

I can't remember how long
the fire's been cooled,
& my legs are twitching more today.
Stomach too moans more than hunger;
I'm afraid.

Lying here the shadows make shapes
with my hand. The storm
is subsiding. There's a cricket
under the bed.

DAY OF CHANGE

My name is June
Bug. I feel splitting

bamboo when the wind
hits. My legs cannot

smooth to the flight
of birds. I want soon

for this chamber
to pass. I need the length

of the snake. I have
seen so much.

two/THE EXECUTRIX OF WEIRDS

for Ray Wiegert
& Jim Sprouse

PORTRAIT: MY AMERICAN MAN
FALL, 1967

to Paul Friedman

Sweat beads the fuzz
on my nose.
I feel pimples swell.
In the booth
behind my ears
a young girl with no pants
hawks
her dream. Dust
from her mother's petticoats
chokes
the light.

I have strong need.
Visions
have passed me by.
I can't write poetry, but my wife
is negro
            & nightly
the same green centipede
wades
into my sleep.

SELF-PORTRAIT IN CAPTIVITY

Binturongs at my back
I stare through mesh
to the aviary
across the sky-blue tile floor

Day's last sun
off a sleeping toucan
frees words
makes white my song

But sweet milk sours
as evening falls jade
over the mandrill's soft clucks
rising hard

to its mate

GODDESS OF THE WHARF

I see her
perched below on the rocks
grown white
out of waste
a great toadstool

Where she is
all
is tactile

time

funneled
by her vortex
bigger
        (blue-fleshed
than death

a lost butterfly shrieks!

   She hoards
   every last sound.

There is no leaving
without
her contract   round
contract
            whirling edge toothed
with signatures
                        loved ones
in blood
              BLOOD

for a

transcendance
a dance
a strange
circular gathering
behind
of the eyes   ears   this palsied

tongue!

THE EXECUTRIX

The executrix of weirds

approaches   Her seepage
spins along a rat's

nerves   It slavers
It eyes my body with

madness   Her fingers goad
the walls

I am gathered-up
Dust-balls move   un-

covering roaches
Their backs glisten

It is the end   She
is pleased

DREAM OF A LIBRARY

Across grey carpet
her long curls reach
the boy
with musk.

Now a teenager lopes by
in a green sweatshirt,
CATBITE NORMAL inked in red
over his chest.

His inner ear clicks.

The four of us
are alone
in a laundromat.
Beyond a metal magazine-rack
the dirty window
fails.

I want to save the life
of a yellow kitten.

Catbite kicks
the boy
in his tiny
pink balls. She covers my face
with her moist.
There are deeper shades of blue than
the backs
of her eyes.

The boy thinks of his mother
& how he can't wake up.

We sin. Our lust forms
a chain. We writhe
on the rug.

LOVE'S BODY CONSUMED

Out beyond
unused skins &
rows
of bed-springs rusting

on plains of ice

lay naked sons
mouths
quaking no blood sound.

Fingers locked
angels
& underworld beasts
rut
their circle tighter

perform unholy
more
than circumcision

cleave
& carry off

to bronze clicking
to his mandibles
they dance

the Father feeding.

SHE DREAMS THE PELVIS

Shackled

her wail
a stairway
circling down
the dream

her flesh
spittle-flecked
shimmers

& the pelvis

out of control
plunges

between white thighs
locked
the bannister slicks

a razor

PARALYSIS

His fingers
splayed
sink deep
to the shudder

that kills

No dream
this beast
floods her throat

Love this thick

a kindness
when it leaves the lids

can close

THE VETERAN

A dry sense of dread
keeps him in bed
not going to work
not shaving
not watering the begonias

now
slim crawling light
                    he's sure
they hive,
            SPIDERS
in a crack
near his pillow,
near his ears

wonders
what he's harbored
what poisons
for years / & god he's frightened
of the raking sun!

    this fourth-year sun
    off the fat pink belly
    of a puppy he's drowned

        his sister's
        fat puppy
        belly-up
        in a pond.

THE BAKER

The Baker
fascinated by a dream
of sea-horses
awoke late

Unkneaded
the sourdough sprouted
yellow pods
took to the air

Entering the shop
the last bits of his life
flashed by
in the jaws of hornets
smelling of mold

A BLIND MAN

I am blind
fondling
legless spiders
& the ant-spattered hammer,
mouth dripping with the custard
of a toad's brain.

The smell of piss on clinkers
tickles my nose.
I wish I could eat glass.

If my god would make me
a mattress of pubez,
& present an earthen jug filled
with the cool
of seaweed
& fresh mushrooms

to soothe my hot eyes

I would lie quietly
& forget all this.

three/THE EMPTY BREAD-BOX HAS A RED EDGE

for Anselm & Gail Parlatore

COLD NIGHT

The cold night has dawned
with more than
the thin
spiders
& snake-foam
I expected. But the beer
tastes like
springtime
& the stars are precious
as my first rug.

I SOLD A POEM

You turn from me.

It's just
a normal night, we did
run out of ice,
& just perhaps
it was the trash I meant
but then forgot
to dump. I kissed your nose
the way I always do.
I agreed I should
have come home sooner. You know
I sold a poem;
you said you understood.
I would have
called
but my mouth was cold with beer.

It's no big thing.

I'm near you now, & you concede
that certain times
in certain ways
I must be free.

You understand.
I understand.
                    But god,

tonight you turn from me.

DIVIDE AGAIN

My wife yearns
to know & have
in unknown & wet streets
the sun

She would strum
few chords, but listen
attentively

Zeus, divide again
my parts
& render me
city

The warmth will come
of itself.

THE MARRIAGE

I am a turtle
with a lead shell,
with fragile blue wings
of gossamer
& small.
The sky is far
when you say you're through.

You are a bobcat
with thin claws of glass,
with grey dreamy eyes
of no luster.
The green tall trees
are emery
when I say I don't love you.

Night comes.
The air is sparse,
the ground cold.
Our eyes round owls
afraid in the dark.
Give me your hand,
it will hold us.

MEMENTOS

Our kitten
"The Brandy Quim"
attempts with passion to
kill
the cardboard box
I brought home
to hold my
personal effects.

She learns its ways

& finally
as if to say "now this
is mine!"
drags her prized rawhide strip
to a chewed corner
sprawls it under her &
haunches down.

I think when I leave
tomorrow
I'll take along that
rawhide strip
so beaten
so embellished with
her hours

& maybe some small thing
belonging to my wife.

BAREFOOT LOVER

This morning
a loaded moving-van bound west
crushed
the apricot pits
you spit
to my street
while strolling with your lover
last night

How they burn my feet

DISTILLED

Supernatural ice-
thaw tears
pierce my skin.

Pores

feel your fingers
ply me
with spirits,
running straight to veins.

It's you
I meet in spring rain.

I'm your still.

I spill clear
your ruddy mixtures

your flame
from my choked eyes
drips down

quenching flowers
at my feet.

ABANDONED

The loneliness
of the night-watchman
wandering heaven's corridors–
knowing there'll be no pay,
no mouths
to feed.

The irony
of the poet
who feels his silence
is misunderstood.

Look love,
Death walks slowly
with an empty satchel.
Our brittle bliss
has no value
for him.

NOTES FOR AN ELEGY

How much easier
   at my window
to be without passion
now winter has come

& the dreadful need
that pushed me late madly to dance
is cold.

Wind shifts grey
without pleasure
in the oaks.

The moon climbs
weary & desperate this design
out of the brush
near the J. Ville Creek.

SNOW ANGEL

Outside my window
a small girl staggers
with the weight
of a hunk of snow. Now
she is breaking it
against a tree. My hands
are cold.

Outside the window
the same girl now
is on her back, she moves
first one leg then
the other, first one arm
then all at once
an angel!

There are angels covering
the lawn. Where their thighs
divide
the green grass pushes
for sun. My winter
is melting. Pieces of angels
break against my limbs.

YELLOW SPRING

Everything outside
is yellow. A crater
in the sidewalk
left by the come
& go of winter, daily
fills up
with popsicle sticks.
When she passes
the air this side my window
crackles, everything, the empty
bread-box has a red edge.
This color is me.
She smiles into the sun
above the house.
She is innocent.
I want fiercely to touch her.